ALL ABOUT BIRDS

ALL ABOUT BIRDS

Sarah Whittley

NEW HOLLAND

First published in 2008 by New Holland Publishers (UK) Ltd
London • Cape Town • Sydney • Auckland

www.newhollandpublishers.com

Garfield House, 86-88 Edgware Road, London W2 2EA, United Kingdom
80 McKenzie Street, Cape Town 8001, South Africa
Unit 1, 66 Gibbes Street, Chatswood, New South Wales, Australia 2067
218 Lake Road, Northcote, Auckland, New Zealand

ISBN 978 1 84773 053 4

Senior Editor: Krystyna Mayer
Design: Fetherstonhaugh (www.fetherstonhaugh.com)
Production: Melanie Dowland
Editorial Consultant: James Parry
Editorial Direction: Rosemary Wilkinson

CONTENTS

INTRODUCTION

The amazing 'courtship dance' of Great Crested Grebes (see page 15) is unmistakeable! The male and female face each other, shake their heads, turn away in a bashful manner and rise up together holding beakfuls of pondweed, a token nesting material.

Birds are great! They are long-lost relations of dinosaurs, and there are over 10,000 different types or species in the world. They aren't all in this book, of course. Here you will find the species you are most likely to see in different habitats in Britain.

In order to find the various species in this book, you'll have to turn into a detective, working out where they live and what they like to eat. Once you have cracked this, not only should you be able to find them, but also, with a little experience, you'll soon know their names.

How to identify birds

Telling one bird from another can be very difficult, even for experts. However, with some help and lots of practice, finding and identifying birds can be great fun – in fact, it can become a real adventure. The first thing to look at is a bird's size. Try to compare it with a common bird you already know, like a pigeon for example. The next thing to check is its bill shape, then whether it has any particular markings and whether it is moving or behaving in a particular way. Don't forget that the colour of a bird's legs can be important.

Basic bird parts
Just like us, birds have names for the different parts of their bodies. It helps to know these names when it comes to describing a bird. For example, the Great Spotted Woodpecker has a red mark on its nape, while the Goldcrest has yellow on its crown.

When it comes to identification, a bird's shape and behaviour can sometimes be more important than its colours, which can change in different light. A Blackbird and a Starling can look similar, but a Starling is thinner and has a very busy, jerky walk and run, whereas a Blackbird is chunkier and will cock its tail and droop its wings. Next time you see these birds, watch their behaviour and see for yourself how they differ.

WHERE BIRDS LIVE

Just like us, birds can be quite fussy about where they live. Every species has its favourite type of home, called a habitat. You wouldn't expect to find the same types of bird at the seaside that you'd get in a forest. However, because birds fly and can move around, don't be surprised if a Sparrowhawk zooms past you in a town or if you see a seagull inland.

Worldwide, there are many different habitats favoured by birds. In Britain, the various habitats can be grouped into the following.

Coast
Beaches, estuaries, mudflats, marshes, coastal lagoons, cliffs and islands.

Mountain and Moors
Any uplands, not just mountains and moors. 'Uplands' simply means land that is high up and not at sea level.

Heathland
Flat and open landscapes with plants such as heather and gorse.

Farmland
Fields, meadows, grasslands and hedgerows.

Wetland
Streams, rivers, lakes, reservoirs, marshland and even ponds in parks and gardens.

Gardens
A variety of gardens may be found in villages, towns, cities and parks.

Woodland
Deciduous and coniferous types of woodland.

TYPES OF BIRD

There are many species of bird in the world – so many that it would be impossible for us and especially scientists to talk about them if they weren't all named and organized. Thanks to a Swedish man called Carl Linnaeus, we now have a classification system for all living things, including birds. The study of naming things is called 'taxonomy', and in the 1750s Carl Linnaeus set up a system for birds that we still use today.

Birds are grouped into families. Some have many species, like the sparrow and weaver family, which has over 140 species worldwide. But other families comprise as few as one species, like the Osprey. Bird types featured in this book include:

Wildfowl

Birds of prey

Pigeons

Larks

Tits

Sparrows

Woodpeckers

Wagtails

Heron

Gamebirds

Waders

Owls

Thrushes

Crows

Finches

Pipits

Cuckoo

Cormorant

Osprey

10 AMAZING FACTS ABOUT BIRDS

1 If you like dinosaurs, you should love birds. Scientists believe that birds are the living descendants of dinosaurs.

2 Some birds, like swans and albatrosses, choose a partner and stay together for the rest of their lives.

3 The Goldcrest is the smallest bird in Europe.

4 The smallest bird in the world is the Bee Hummingbird. It's 6.2 centimetres long and weighs 1.6 grams. Its eggs are the size of a little finger's fingernail.

5 The fastest-flying bird in the world is the Peregrine Falcon. One was recorded flying at 145 kilometres an hour, but some people claim it can fly as fast as 320 kilometres an hour.

6 The Ostrich is the biggest living bird in the world. It grows up to 2.7 metres tall. It's also the fastest bird on land and can run at a speed of up to 70 kilometres an hour.

7 The highest-flying bird in the world is a Rüppell's Griffon Vulture. One was recorded travelling at a height of 11,278 metres.

8 The Wandering Albatross has the longest wingspan of any bird in the world. It measures a huge 4 metres.

9 Some parrots can live to up to 100 years of age.

10 The Harpy Eagle is thought to be the biggest bird of prey in the world. An adult has a wingspan of 2.1 metres, and it can snatch prey as large as monkeys out of trees.

Camouflage A way of hiding something by blending it in with the background.

Carnivorous Having a meat-eating diet.

Carrion Meat from dead animals.

Conifers Trees that don't lose their leaves in winter.

Courtship Type of behaviour that leads to mating.

Crustaceans Animals with hard shells, jointed legs and segmented bodies – like crabs and lobsters.

Deciduous trees Trees that lose their leaves in autumn.

Display Show put on to attract a mate.

Feral Becoming wild after being tamed.

Fledgling Young bird that has just left the nest.

Habitat Area where an animal may live.

Iridescent Showing rainbow-like colours that seem to change.

Larva Newly hatched animal, usually an insect. If there's more than one, the word changes to larvae.

Leatherjackets The larvae of the crane-fly insect.

Lek A gathering of males of certain animal species, including birds like the Dunnock (see page 48), in which they engage in competitive mating displays.

Metallic Sounding or looking like metal.

Molluscs Animals with hard or soft shells and unsegmented bodies, such as slugs and snails.

Nestling Baby bird that is still in the nest.

Omnivorous Having a diet of both vegetables and animals.

Plumage Covering of feathers on a bird.

Range Extent of area where species is found.

Roost Place where birds sleep.

Sickle Hand-tool with a semi-circular blade, used for cutting tall grass.

Sociable Liking the company of other birds.

Territorial Defending an area from intruders.

Uplands Area of high or hilly land.

MUTE SWAN
CYGNUS OLOR

When to see All year round.

Where to see Slow-moving water, lakes, ditches, canals and rivers.

What to look for An enormous white bird with a long and graceful neck and orange bill. On water swans look very elegant, but on land they appear clumsy, waddling along on their big webbed feet. 125–155 cm.

What they eat Vegetation from land and water, insects and snails. They can reach a long way down into the water with their long necks, sometimes up-ending completely.

Did you know?
This is Europe's largest bird. Although it is generally silent, it hisses and snorts when angry or disturbed. Baby swans are called cygnets. Normally they are grey in colour, but very rarely they can be snow white.

Juvenile

Adult

MALLARD
ANAS PLATYRHYNCHOS

When to see All year round.

Where to see Slow-flowing water, ponds, lakes, rivers, parks and ditches.

What to look for Britain's most familiar duck. The males have dark, shiny green heads, thin white collars, yellow bills, chestnut breasts and grey sides. The females are an intricate blend of dark and light brown with a darker stripe through the eye. 50–65 cm.

What they eat Vegetation, seeds and insects from land and water. Mallards often up-end in water to reach their food. They also like feeding on bread along rivers and in parks.

Did you know?

Pure-bred wild Mallards aren't as common as you might think. Many farmyard ducks have interbred with Mallards, producing a wide variety of colours and shapes.

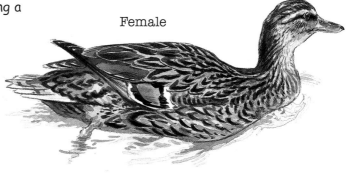

Female

Male

TUFTED DUCK
AYTHYA FULIGULA

Did you know?
Tufted Ducks can dive as deep as 609 cm – that's as big a distance as the length of a large caravan!

When to see All year round.

Where to see Lakes, reservoirs, rivers, coastal lagoons and ponds.

What to look for The males are all black with a hint of purple and clean white sides. They have a flowing crest from the back of the head. The females are dark brown with pale brown sides. 40–47 cm.

What they eat They like to dive for their food, paddling furiously underwater to catch insects, shrimps, larvae and mussels. They also eat pondweed.

Female

Male

GREAT CRESTED GREBE
PODICEPS CRISTATUS

When to see All year round.

Where to see Lakes, large ponds, estuaries and rivers.

What to look for In their spectacular summer plumage, with head tufts and neck frills – you can't mistake them! In winter the head is plain white with a black cap. In Britain this species was once killed for its head plumes, which were used to decorate women's hats. It was reduced to 42 pairs in 1860, but has been protected for many years and has greatly increased in both numbers and range. 45–46 cm.

What they eat Mainly fish, but also small amphibians and aquatic larvae.

Did you know?
When courting grebes dance with one another, it looks like Olympic synchronized swimming – but instead of getting a medal at the end, they dangle bits of pondweed in front of each other! (See page 6 for more about this.)

Boldly marked chicks often hitch a lift on parents' backs.

GREY HERON
ARDEA CINEREA

Did you know?

A heron's loud, harsh call sounds as though it is saying 'Frank'.

When to see All year round.

Where to see Anywhere near water: lakes, marshes, rivers and estuaries. Roosts and nests in trees.

What to look for A large grey bird with a very long neck and legs, and a long, dagger-shaped bill. It often sits very still by water with its neck outstretched, ready to stab at its prey. When flying it keeps its neck tucked in, and looks a bit like a pterosaur! 90–98 cm.

What they eat A varied diet, mainly of fish, but also including amphibians and even small mammals and birds.

OSPREY
PANDION HALIAETUS

Did you know?
When fishing an Osprey can hit the water at almost 80 kph. It uses its long legs and sharp talons to grab fish from the water.

When to see Ospreys spend the winter in Africa, visiting Europe between March and September.

Where to see Usually near water sites such as lakes and coastal lagoons. Ospreys often sit on perches in or next to water.

What to look for A large dark brown and white bird with narrow wings. It can look like a big seagull from a distance, but note the thick black eye-stripe. 55–58 cm.

What they eat Mainly fish.

MOORHEN
GALLINULA CHLOROPUS

Did you know?

Moorhens are fiercely territorial, sometimes fighting each other by jumping up and kicking out with their long legs. They will also chase off most intruders.

When to see All year round.

Where to see Never too far from water – lakes, rivers, ditches, ponds, gardens and farmland.

What to look for A black bird with a red shield above its bill, a white line on its sides and longish green-yellow legs and toes. Its pointy tail constantly flicks as it moves, revealing a white under-tail. 32–35 cm.

What they eat Food from water and land, snails, fish, worms, weeds, seeds and insects.

Adult

Parents are highly devoted to their odd-looking chicks, which have semi-bald red heads!

Juvenile

COOT
FULICA ATRA

Coots may congregate in groups outside the breeding season.

Juvenile

Adult

Did you know?

They have really weird-looking feet! Next time you see one check them out: they're semi-webbed with long toenails. Like Moorhens, they can be aggressive towards other birds (including much larger swans!), particularly during the breeding season.

When to see All year round.

Where to see Lakes, reservoirs, rivers and gravel pits. They prefer bigger ponds than Moorhens.

What to look for A rounded black bird, similar to a Moorhen but slightly larger and with no red on its face. Instead it has a white bill with a large white shield on its forehead. 36–38 cm.

What they eat Plants, insects, snails, freshwater mussels and tadpoles.

AVOCET

RECURVIROSTRA AVOSETTA

Juvenile

Adult

When to see All year round.

Where to see Shallow coastal lagoons and marshes. In Britain, mainly coastlines of East Anglia, Kent and the south-west.

What to look for An unmistakable long-legged bird with black-and-white plumage and a surprisingly long bill that turns up towards the end. 42–45 cm.

What they eat Avocets swing their bills from side to side in the water to gather shrimps, worms, crustaceans, sandhoppers and larvae to eat.

Did you know?
The Royal Society for the Protection of Birds (RSPB) uses this bird as its logo.

CURLEW

NUMENIUS ARQUATA

Did you know?
One other bird, the Whimbrel, looks very similar, but it is not as common as the Curlew in Britain.

When to see All year round.

Where to see Uplands, moors, open fields, estuaries and marshes across Britain.

What to look for A large brown wader with a very long, downwards-curving bill. This is Europe's biggest wader. 50–60 cm.

What they eat Using its long bill, the Curlew probes the ground in search of crabs, lugworms, ragworms, snails, shrimps, insects, beetle larvae and spiders.

KINGFISHER
ALCEDO ATTHIS

When to see All year round.

Where to see Near to rivers, streams, ponds and canals.

What to look for A dazzling bird of electric blues, greens and reds, often seen dashing along a river at high speed emitting a piercing, short sharp call. It looks somewhat top heavy due to its large bill and big head. Kingfishers nest in burrows that they excavate in sandy soil on stream banks. The nest tunnel is up to 90 cm long, with a nest chamber at the end. 16–17 cm.

What they eat Small fish and aquatic insects.

Did you know?
They are great hunters, often sitting still for hours waiting for a fish to swim by and then suddenly dropping down like an arrow to snap up their prey.

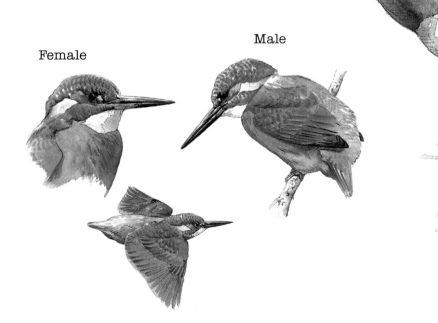

Female

Male

GREYLAG GOOSE
ANSER ANSER

Did you know?

Most domestic (farmyard) geese are bred from this bird, and it is Europe's most common goose.

When to see All year round.

Where to see Lakes, reservoirs, fields, farmland, rivers and parks.

What to look for A chunky grey-brown goose with subtle barring on its sides, white under its tail, thick orange bill and paler orange legs. When alarmed it raises it head and lifts its bill in a threatening manner. 75–90 cm.

What they eat Completely vegetarian, feeding in water and on land. Eats seeds, pondweed, plants, grasses, roots and leaves.

CANADA GOOSE
BRANTA CANADENSIS

When to see All year round.

Where to see Lakes, reservoirs, rivers, farmland fields, parks and moors.

What to look for A large goose with a brown body, black neck and head with a white chin-strap. It can be seen in rivers and large ponds, as well as in flocks grazing on grass in fields. Canada Geese fly in a perfect 'V' formation. 56–110 cm.

What they eat Lots of different weeds, seeds, grasses and fruits.

Did you know?

Scientists believe that Canada Geese have up to 13 different calls for saying things like hello, giving warnings, expressing contentment and scolding. They were introduced to Britain from North America and have spread widely.

CORMORANT
PHALACROCORAX CARBO

Did you know?
There is another bird that looks very similar, called a Shag, but it is found only in coastal areas.

Continental European race

Juvenile

Adult

When to see All year round.

Where to see Coasts, estuaries, rivers and lakes.

What to look for A tall dark bird with a long neck and a back that looks scaly. It looks like a cross between a reptile and a pterodactyl (a flying dinosaur)! It often sits with its bill up and its wings outstretched to dry. Cormorants always fly with their necks stretched out. They sit very low on the water so that sometimes only the tops of their backs and their necks are visible. 80–10 cm.

What they eat All sorts of fish, including eels and flat fish.

OYSTERCATCHER

HAEMATOPUS OSTRALEGUS

When to see All year round.

Where to see Coastal habitats, inland reservoirs, gravel pits and marshes.

What to look for A black-and-white wader with a long orange-red bill and legs, and a red eye. In winter it has a white chin-strap. You'll probably hear Oystercatchers before you see them as they are easily excited, uttering loud piping 'kleep, kleep' calls. 40–45 cm.

What they eat Shellfish such as mussels, and crabs and worms.

Did you know?

Oystercatchers will fiercely defend their nests and chicks. If anything, including humans, gets too close, you can expect an aerial attack and a nasty peck!

Summer

Winter

REDSHANK

TRINGA TOTANUS

Winter

Did you know?

The Redshank gets its name from the colour of its legs. The word shank means leg.

Summer

When to see All year round.

Where to see Coasts, marshes, moors, inland reservoirs and gravel pits.

What to look for Red legs! The Redshank's long red legs mark it out from the other brown-coloured waders in Britain. The Spotted Redshank also has red legs, but it is much rarer, only visiting Britain in winter and on migration. 27–29 cm.

What they eat Shrimps, crustaceans, molluscs and, when further inland, worms, bugs and spiders.

BLACK-HEADED GULL
LARUS RIDIBUNDUS

Did you know?

Their heads are actually chocolate brown in colour.

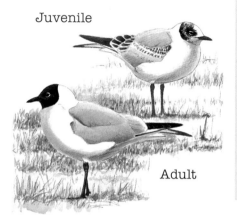

Juvenile

Adult

When to see All year round.

Where to see Many different coastal and inland habitats, including rubbish dumps and inland fields, especially when they are being ploughed. You can even find them in cities.

What to look for A gull with dark red legs, pale grey back and dark tips on its wings. It only has a dark hood in summer. In winter it is white with two dark smudges on either side of its head. 27–29 cm.

What they eat Almost anything! They'll even visit bird tables.

GREAT BLACK-BACKED GULL
LARUS MARINUS

Did you know?

Over a hundred years ago this bird was nearly extinct in Britain, but now its numbers have increased.

Adult

Juveniles

When to see All year round.

Where to see They breed near coasts, but will also venture inland to visit rubbish tips and often roost at reservoirs.

What to look for A massive gull (Europe's largest), bigger than a buzzard, with black back, yellow bill and pink-brown legs. 64–78 cm.

What they eat Anything that moves! Small mammals, fish, frogs and carrion.

COMMON TERN
STERNA HIRUNDO

Juvenile

When to see Summer visitors to Britain from April to September.

Where to see Around coasts, but also on lakes and rivers.

What to look for Similar to a seagull but smaller and more dainty and agile, with pointed wings. Their long forked tail has earned them the nickname 'sea-swallow'. In summer the bill is red with a black tip; in winter it is black. The birds fly gracefully and frequently hover over water before plunging for a fish. 30–35 cm.

What they eat Mainly small fish, sand eels and shrimps, plus insects and larvae.

Adult

Did you know?
Because they breed on sandy and shingle beaches around the coast, walkers can easily stand on and destroy their camouflaged eggs.

Adult

Juvenile

SANDWICH TERN
STERNA SANDVICENSIS
Although these beautiful birds breed in only a few places in coastal England, they explore widely with their vociferous young once they have fledged and can be seen on many beaches. 41 cm.

27

PUFFIN
FRATERCULA ARCTICA

Did you know?
Puffins make their nests in burrows, which they either dig themselves or borrow from rabbits. They don't reach breeding age until they are 5–6 years old. Their scientific name means 'little brother from the Arctic'.

When to see Easiest to see when they are breeding from March to August.

Where to see Rocky islands and cliffs around the coast.

What to look for A small bird with a black back, white front, bright orange legs and huge, flat multicoloured bill, making it look top-heavy. Puffins' eye markings make them look sad. The birds live together in colonies, and often have a lifespan of 20 years. 26–29 cm.

What they eat Small fish, especially sandeels. The huge bill comes into use when they are feeding young as they can cram lots of fish into it.

GREY PARTRIDGE
PERDIX PERDIX

When to see All year round.

Where to see Farmland and open countryside. Not found in mountainous habitats.

What to look for A shy dumpy bird with a rust-coloured head, greyish front, chestnut tail and dark patch on its belly. The female lacks or has a very small belly patch. The bird tip-toes nervously on the ground, and if spotted prefers to sit still rather than fly. 29–31 cm.

What they eat Seeds, leaves, grasses and insects.

Did you know?
This once-common species is now becoming rarer – its numbers halved between the 1960s and 1990s.

RED-LEGGED PARTRIDGE
ALECTORIS RUFA

When to see All year round.

Where to see Open farmland and occasionally rough land in towns.

What to look for A colourful, exotic-looking bird similar in size to a moorhen. The bold stripes on its flanks, its red bill and legs, and the red around its eye make it look very different from the Grey Partridge. 34 cm.

What they eat Seeds, grain, berries and insects when feeding young.

Did you know?
It was introduced from France to Britain in the 1700s as a game bird, hence its alternative name, the French Partridge.

PHEASANT
PHASIANUS COLCHICUS

Males

When to see All year round.

Where to see Farmland, woodland and large gardens.

What to look for The male is a spectacular, exotic-looking copper-coloured bird with a dark green head, bright red face wattles, ear tufts and very long tail. The shy female is brown.

To impress the females, the males puff up their feathers and drum their wings. 53–89 cm.

What they eat A variety of insects, seeds, worms, berries and plants.

Female with chicks

Did you know?

Pheasants aren't native to Europe. They come from China and were introduced to England in the 11th century by the Normans.

COMMON BUZZARD
BUTEO BUTEO

When to see All year round.

Where to see Farmland, moors, woodlands and hilly areas.

What to look for In flight they have broad wings with finger-like feather tips. They can be different shades of brown, from very dark brown to almost cream. Some people confuse them with eagles, but eagles are much bigger. They sometimes fly holding their wings in a shallow 'V' shape. 51–57 cm.

What they eat Small mammals like voles and rabbits, and also birds such as young pigeons and crows.

Dark variety

Did you know?
The Buzzard is Britain's most common bird of prey.

Very pale variety

KESTREL
FALCO TINNUNCULUS

Did you know?
The Kestrel is the only bird you'll see in Britain that hovers for a long time.

Juvenile

When to see All year round.

Where to see Many grassland habitats, including large gardens, roadsides and farmland.

What to look for A smartly dressed falcon. The male has a chestnut back, wings with dark tips, grey head and tail with a black band at the end. The female is less colourful. In flight Kestrels look more delicate than Sparrowhawks and have thinner and more pointed wings. They have very good eyesight and 'hover hunt', flying in one place and then diving for their food. 32–35 cm.

What they eat Voles and other small mammals, insects, worms and small birds.

Male

Female

LAPWING
VANELLUS VANELLUS

When to see All year round.

Where to see Fields with short grass, marshes, bogs and other open areas.

What to look for A large plover with a splendid dark crest that sweeps out from the back of its head, iridescent dark green back, black breast and white belly. In winter and autumn Lapwings form large flocks, which are sometimes joined by Golden Plovers. 28–31 cm.

What they eat A mixture of bugs and some vegetation – spiders, worms, caterpillars, leatherjackets and even small frogs. Sometimes they'll repeatedly tap their feet on the ground to encourage insects to the surface.

Did you know?
They are also called Peewits due to their distinctive drawn-out 'peee-wit' call.

CUCKOO
CUCULUS CANORUS

Female –
grey version

Male

When to see A summer visitor from March to August.

Where to see Many rural habitats, but not towns.

What to look for With their grey backs, long tails and pointy wings, cuckoos can look like small birds of prey, especially in flight. Some females are a rust (or rufous) colour instead of grey, but all birds have barred undersides. 32–34 cm.

What they eat Insects including the scary-looking hairy caterpillars, as well as eggs and even baby birds from nests.

Did you know?
Cuckoos don't make a nest or bring up their young. Instead, they lay an egg in another bird's nest and let it do all the hard work!

Female –
rufous version

WOODPIGEON
COLUMBA PALUMBUS

When to see All year round.

Where to see Farmland, woodland, parks, gardens and cities.

What to look for A large, chubby grey pigeon with a pink-rose-coloured breast. It has a white and green patch on its neck. Look for a white patch on both wings when it is flying. It makes an unmistakeable loud clattering noise with its wings when it flies up from a tree. 40–42 cm.

What they eat Mainly vegetarian but will eat insects, especially when it is feeding young.

Adult

Juvenile

Did you know?
They can easily be confused with Stock Doves, but Woodpigeons always show white patches in their wings when flying.

LITTLE OWL
ATHENE NOCTUA

Did you know?
Although small, the Little Owl is clever and brave, so much so that Athena, the Greek goddess of war, used it as her mascot.

When to see All year round.

Where to see Open countryside, uplands, moors and farmland.

What to look for A small brown owl with cream spots all over and piercing yellow eyes. It can look round and dumpy but stretches up when alarmed, which makes it looks tall and thin. Unlike most owls, it hunts during the day. 21–23 cm.

What they eat Insects, worms and small mammals such as voles and shrews. If necessary, it will run along the ground to catch its prey.

MEADOW PIPIT
ANTHUS PRATENSIS

When to see All year round.

Where to see Open countryside, fields, marshes and upland moors.

What to look for An LBJ (little brown job!), but with lovely brown streaks all over. It has a dark olive-brown streaked back, pale buff streaked breast and pink legs. There are no marks on its cheeks and it has a thin bill. 14 cm.

What they eat Insects and spiders, and sometimes seeds.

Winter

Summer

Did you know?
Its song flight is a little similar to the Skylark's, but it doesn't fly as high. It parachutes down to the ground with its wings half open.

SKYLARK
ALAUDA ARVENSIS

Did you know?
The Skylark flies incredibly high in the sky, singing as it ascends until you can only see a tiny dot. It then falls through the air like a parachute, speeding up before it reaches the ground. This is called a song flight.

When to see All year round.

Where to see Farmlands, grasslands, marshes and uplands.

What to look for Another LBJ, with intricate brown streaks and mottling. It sometimes raises its crest if excited. Listen for its complex, busy warbling song. 18–19 cm.

What they eat Insects and plants, especially weeds and seeds.

CARRION CROW
CORVUS CORONE

Crows will mob birds that they see as threats, like this buzzard.

When to see All year round.

Where to see Farmland, open countryside, coastal habitats and towns.

What to look for A chunky black bird with a large dark bill and grey legs. In flight its wings have 'fingers', making it look similar to a buzzard. It is less likely to gather in large numbers, like Rooks do. 45–47 cm.

What they eat Almost anything! Insects, mammals, birds – dead or alive! Also seeds, fruit, shellfish and plants.

Carrion Crow

Did you know?

The Hooded Crow, *Corvus cornix*, is a close relative. It replaces the Carrion Crow in northern parts of Britain and continental Europe.

Hooded Crow

JACKDAW
CORVUS MONEDULA

When to see All year round.

Where to see Many places, from gardens and farmland to towns and cliffs.

What to look for A small crow with grey on the sides and back of its head and very pale grey eyes. It has a jerky walk, interrupted with hops, and can even hop sideways. 33–34 cm.

What they eat Almost anything! Their normal diet consists of insects, fruit including berries, seeds, kitchen scraps and carrion. They will also visit bird tables.

Nests in holes mainly in trees and buildings

Did you know?
These intelligent birds love to nest in holes, especially chimney pots, and will even make use of old rabbit burrows for their nests.

SPARROWHAWK
ACCIPITER NISUS

Juvenile

Did you know?

Sparrowhawks can run down their prey like dinosaurs, grabbing it with their long legs and sharp talons.

When to see All year round.

Where to see Many habitats, including gardens and woodland across Britain and continental Europe.

What to look for A powerful bird of prey with broad rounded wings and long barred tail. The barring on its chest is obvious, and so too are its yellow legs. 28–38 cm.

What they eat Not just sparrows, although 98 per cent of its diet is small birds.

Female

TAWNY OWL
STRIX ALUCO

Adult

When to see All year round – this is Britain's most common owl.

Where to see Mature trees in parks, woodland, towns and countryside across Europe.

What to look for A brown owl about the size of a Woodpigeon. It has big brown eyes and its plumage is covered in lots of intricate markings. Although it's unusual to see it during the day, you can sometimes notice the fluffy fledglings sitting in trees. 37–39 cm.

What they eat Small mammals such as mice and voles, small birds and some insects.

Fledgling

Did you know?

The Tawny Owl has been known to snatch fish from garden ponds.

COLLARED DOVE
STREPTOPELIA DECAOCTO

Did you know?
These birds are taking over the world!
They originated in Central Asia, but now
they are also found in Europe and
America – and they're still spreading.

Adult

Juvenile

When to see All year round.

Where to see Almost anywhere near
humans! Villages, towns and farmland.

What to look for An exquisite dainty,
sandy-pink-coloured dove with a black
line running almost around its neck.
(It's not actually a collar.) They're
usually seen in pairs, and if you get
close enough you will see their red eyes.
31–33 cm.

What they eat Principally vegetation, including seeds and fruits, but also
some insects.

FERAL PIGEON
COLUMBA LIVIA

When to see All year round.

Where to see Everywhere! Especially common near humans, in cities, villages, farmland and parks.

What to look for Smaller than a Woodpigeon, and more like a Collared Dove in shape and size. Colours vary and include greys, whites and browns. Feral Pigeons can become very tame. 31–34 cm.

What they eat Insects and seeds.

Did you know?

Feral Pigeons are descended from Rock Doves, which still exist today and live on coastal cliffs. The have grey backs with dark bands on their wings, grey heads and purple-green necks.

Courting male (in foreground) with female

HOUSE MARTIN
DELCHON URBICA

Sometimes nests near other species, such as House Sparrows.

When to see March to October.

Where to see Found around buildings and farmyards, on telephone wires, in open countryside and on coastal cliffs.

What to look for Similar in shape to a Swallow, but smaller and with an obvious white rump and short forked tail but no streamers. The back is blue-black, while the front, (including the chin) is white. Watch House Martins make their cup-shaped mud nests under the eaves on buildings. 12–13 cm.

What they eat Flying insects.

Did you know?

There's another bird that looks very similar called a Sand Martin, but it has a brown back and lacks the white rump.

SWIFT
APUS APUS

When to see April to August.

Where to see Always in the sky unless nesting, in which case on cliffs or buildings across Europe.

What to look for Similar to a Swallow but larger and dark all over (except for the pale chin), with long, stiff sickle-shaped wings. Groups of Swifts often zoom around buildings, screaming as they fly. 16–17 cm.

What they eat Flying insects. They can catch up to 10,000 insects in just one day!

Did you know?

This bird is amazing! It spends most of its life on the wing, only landing to nest. It sleeps, mates and eats on the wing.

SWALLOW
HIRUNDO RUSTICA

When to see March to October.

Where to see Open countryside, farmyards, telephone wires and villages.

What to look for In flight a dark blue-black back and white front with a red face and chin. No white rump but long forked tail feathers. When perched Swallows look long, due to their tail streamers. If you can, get a close-up look – they're stunning! 17–19 cm.

What they eat Flying insects.

Did you know?

In the past people believed that Swallows dug holes in mud and hibernated underground – which of course they don't! In winter they go to Africa.

GREAT SPOTTED WOODPECKER
DENDROCOPOS MAJOR

Did you know?

In winter or early spring they use branches to drum on, marking territory and hoping to attract a mate.

When to see All year round.

Where to see Anywhere where there are trees!

What to look for A stonking blackbird-sized, black-and-white bird with flashes of red. Both sexes have red vents, but only the male has a red patch on the back of its head. The juvenile bird has a red patch on its forehead. 22–23 cm.

What they eat Insects, especially wood-boring insect larvae. They like feeding on peanuts and seeds, and visit birdfeeders to get them.

Male

Juvenile

PIED WAGTAIL
MOTACILLA ALBA

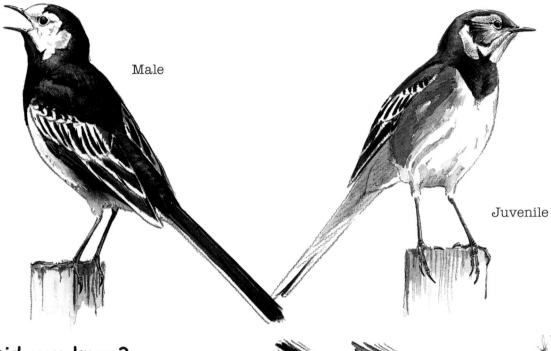

Male

Juvenile

Did you know?
Pied Wagtails can have incredibly large roosts. The largest roost in Britain was 5,000 in a reed bed, but they also roost in towns. When they call they say 'Chiswick'.

Continental form, or White Wagtail

When to see All year round.

Where to see Almost anywhere, from cities to open countryside.

What to look for A sparrow-sized black, white and grey bird with a very long tail that it never stops wagging. On the ground it has a jerky walk, and often breaks into a sudden run as it chases an insect. 18 cm.

What they eat Insects, especially flies and midges.

DUNNOCK
PRUNELLA MODULARIS

Adult

Did you know?
Dunnocks have an amazing courtship. The females rule the roost, sometimes selecting one, two or even three partners from a group (or lek) of 'wing-flicking', displaying males.

When to see
All year round.

Where to see
Gardens, farmland and hedgerows with lots of dense cover.

What to look for
A sparrow-sized bird with a brown-streaked back, blue-grey front and thin, insect-eating bill. It's most likely to be seen on the ground, where it shuffles around looking rather like a mouse. 14–15 cm.

What they eat Mainly insects, but also seeds and berries.

Juvenile

Male Dunnocks put on displays, or leks, to impress females.

WREN
TROGLODYTES TROGLODYTES

When to see All year round.

Where to see Many habitats with trees and low bushes. Gardens, woodland, hedgerows and moors.

What to look for A tiny bird with a big personality! This dinky brown bird with very intricate barring has a restless nature. It nearly always zips around with a cocked tail. For its size it makes amazingly loud noises. It is a brave bird and can upset and even scare off some predators with its 'tic, tic' alarm call. The male is especially active in spring, when he builds several nests for the female to choose from! 9–10 cm.

What they eat Insects and spiders.

As many as 63 Wrens have been found nesting in a nestbox.

Did you know?
In cold weather Wrens will nest communally. Up to a hundred birds have been recorded snuggling up together.

ROBIN
ERITHACUS RUBECULA

Puffs out feathers in cold weather to keep warm – making it look twice its size.

When to see All year round.

Where to see Gardens, woodlands and hedgerows.

What to look for A sparrow-sized bird with a warm brown back, pale belly and blazing bright red chest and face. It often stands upright with drooping wings, hops energetically and then stops suddenly with an indignant flick and bob. 14 cm.

What they eat Bugs, especially worms, and also seeds and berries. Robins often watch gardeners dig, in case they turn up some worms.

Did you know?

If you're patient, you can train Robins to feed from your hand. Just make sure there aren't any cats about!

Adult

Juvenile

Male

BLACKBIRD
TURDUS MERULA

Female

When to see All year round.

Where to see Gardens, parks, woodland, farmland and moors.

What to look for A glossy black bird. The male has a bright yellow eye-ring and bill. The female is brown and occasionally mottled. The Blackbird often sings its beautiful rich, flute-like song from a regular perch. 24–25 cm.

What they eat Mainly carnivorous in summer – insects, tadpoles and even cat food! Otherwise, it eats berries and fruit.

Did you know?
When alarmed or excited the Blackbird has a loud call that ends with a repeated metallic-sounding 'plink, plink, plink'. It also makes this call before roosting.

SONG THRUSH
TURDUS PHILOMELOS

Adult

Did you know?
The Mistle Thrush looks very similar, but is bigger and greyer. Its spots are untidy splodges while those of the Song Thrush are in neat lines.

When to see All year round, but more arrive in Britain from northern Europe in autumn.

Where to see Parks, gardens, woodland and farmland. Never far from trees.

What to look for Just smaller than a Blackbird, with a plain brown back and tail, and arrowhead-shaped spots on a pale belly. 23 cm.

What they eat Bugs, worms, caterpillars and snails. It smashes open snails by banging them against a stone.

Juvenile

51

CHIFFCHAFF
PHYLLOSCOPUS COLLYBITA

Did you know?

Chiffchaffs get their name from their song, which goes 'chiff-chaff, chiff-chaff'. You know spring is on its way when you hear this sound.

Adult

Juvenile

Can be seen collecting insects from undersides of leaves.

When to see All year round, but more arrive for summer from March and leave by September.

Where to see In leafy trees in gardens, parks and woodland.

What to look for A restless Blue Tit-sized bird that flits from leaf to leaf. It has a plain green-brown back and a pale underside that can look yellowish in spring. The eyes have a dark stripe through them and a pale stripe just above. 10–11 cm.

What they eat Insects.

GOLDCREST
REGULUS REGULUS

When to see All year round.

Where to see Parks, gardens and woodlands – anywhere with trees, especially conifers.

What to look for A tiny bird with a yellow stripe with black edges on top of its head. It has a dark green back and a buff front, large eyes and a rather rounded, dumpy body. The darker wings have white wing-bars. Listen out for a high-pitched 'tzi-tzi-tzi' coming from the bushes: that'll be Goldcrests calling to each another. 9 cm.

What they eat Insects, spiders and some seeds. They may occasionally take small crumbs and seeds from bird tables.

Flicks through foliage in search of insects.

Female

Male

Did you know?
This is Europe's smallest bird.

LONG-TAILED TIT
AEGITHALOS CAUDATUS

They fly around in large noisy groups.

Did you know?
Their tiny, elastic ball of a nest expands as the young grow. When it's cold, family groups (sometimes up to 20 birds) cuddle up at night to keep warm.

Adult

When to see All year round.

Where to see Woodland, hedgerows and gardens with trees.

What to look for Fluffy-looking pink-brown balls with long tails. Sometimes it's best to use your ears to locate them! These sociable birds zoom around in large and noisy flocks excitedly screaming a high-pitched 'see, see, see' with a quieter 'thrup, thrup' at the end. 14 cm.

What they eat Insects, spiders and some seeds.

Juvenile

Northern race, found in Scandinavia.

BLUE TIT
PARUS CAERULEUS

Juvenile

When to see All year round.

Where to see Many places with trees – gardens, woodlands and hedgerows.

What to look for A brilliant brightly coloured bird with bags of character that is great to watch. It has a blue forehead and white cheeks with a black line through the eye. Blue Tits are often noisy guests at birdfeeders, squabbling and jostling for the best position. 11.5 cm.

What they eat Insects, especially caterpillars, seeds and nuts.

Did you know?
These tiny birds really feel the freezing winter weather. If they don't eat enough during the day, they may freeze to death at night.

Adult

GREAT TIT
PARUS MAJOR

Juvenile

When to see All year round.

Where to see Many places with trees – gardens, woodlands and hedgerows.

What to look for Similar to the Blue Tit, but bigger (sparrow-sized) and with a black head, white cheeks and an obvious black line running down its yellow belly. Its wings and tail are more grey than blue. 14 cm.

What they eat Insects, but they also love peanuts.

Did you know?
You probably unknowingly hear them all the time. They make a variety of noises, from the familiar 'chink, chink' to a scolding 'chea chea chea' and a see-sawing 'tee-chu, tee-chu'.

Adult

NUTHATCH
SITTA EUROPAEA

Wedges nuts and seeds in bark, then smashes them open with its powerful bill.

Did you know?

This is the only bird in Europe that has the ability to climb down a tree headfirst! Birds like woodpeckers can only go upwards.

When to see All year round.

Where to see Woodland, gardens and parks with mature trees.

What to look for A dramatic bird with no neck! It has a grey back, rust-brown front and black stripe running through its eye. The bandit eye-stripe can make it look rather like a thug! Its large grey bill is designed for hacking through nuts. It nests in holes or crevices, and may reduce the size of an entrance hole by building a neat mud wall. 14 cm.

What they eat
Insects and their larvae, spiders, nuts and seeds. It may come to bird tables, where it can be aggressive and drive away other species.

JAY
GARRULUS GLANDARIUS

When to see All year round, but best in autumn when collecting acorns.

Where to see Woodland, gardens and parks with lots of trees.

What to look for A big brightly coloured bird of the crow family. It has pink-brown feathers, a white forehead with black flecks and an electric blue flash in its wings. 34–35 cm.

What they eat Some insects, but its favourite food is acorns. It hides these in autumn and eats them throughout the year – if it can find them!

Crest is raised during courtship or when annoyed.

Did you know?

Although Jays are big and pink they're very shy. The best time to see them is at dawn.

MAGPIE
PICA PICA

When to see All year round.

Where to see Many habitats including farmland, parks, gardens, moors and coasts.

What to look for An impressive black-and-white bird with a very long, wedge-shaped tail and plenty of attitude! If you look closely you can see purples, blues and greens in its iridescent plumage.
44–46 cm.

What they eat A variety of foods including insects, frogs, mammals, birds and vegetation.

Adult

Did you know?
Magpies are smart. They can even make nests with roofs to keep out the rain.

Juvenile

STARLING
STURNUS VULGARIS

When to see All year round.

Where to see Open grassland, lawns, playing fields and farmland.

What to look for A spectacular bird that you can never tire of watching. Its iridescent dark blue-green plumage is covered with spots in winter. It has a long, yellow dagger-like bill. Starlings are sociable birds that walk with a jerky strut. 21–22 cm.

What they eat Insects, especially leatherjackets (crane-fly larvae), which it plucks out of the ground with its long bill.

Adult summer

Adult winter

Juvenile

Did you know?
These smart copycat birds can mimic other bird calls. What's more, they can even impersonate telephone rings and wolf-whistles!

HOUSE SPARROW
PASSER DOMESTICUS

Did you know?

Although House Sparrows are relatively common, their numbers have recently dropped very quickly. Almost half of London's sparrows have disappeared. Scientists are trying to find out why.

Male

Female

A dust-bath gets rid of parasites and keeps the feathers clean.

When to see All year round.

Where to see Gardens, parks, farms – anywhere near humans.

What to look for Noisy and sociable birds that always look like they're having fun! The female is a mixture of browns with a cream stripe above the eye. The male has a red-brown back with dark markings, a grey crown and cheeks, and a black bib. Sparrows usually nest in holes in buildings and other places. The nests are lined with hairs, string, paper and feathers – which may be plucked from a live pigeon! 14–15 cm.

What they eat Seeds from weeds, peanuts, insects and kitchen scraps. In the days of horses and carts, sparrows ate oats from horses' nosebags.

CHAFFINCH
FRINGILLA COELEBS

Did you know?

The females look very similar to female sparrows. The easiest way to distinguish them is by the Chaffinch's white wing-bar.

When to see All year round.

Where to see Gardens, woodlands – anywhere with trees and bushes.

What to look for The male is a serious contender for Britain's most colourful bird. He has a bright pink front and face, grey crown and nape, and dark wings with an obvious white wing-bar. The female is much less colourful, mainly brown and cream. Both sexes are sparrow-sized. 14–15 cm.

What they eat Mainly seeds, but also insects while breeding.

Male

Female

Chaffinches often feed in groups on the ground.

GREENFINCH
CARDUELIS CHORIS

When to see All year round.

Where to see Farmland, woodland, hedgerows, gardens and parks.

What to look for The male has a dazzling green-yellow breast, a darker olive-green back and a pale pink, thick bill. The wing has a bright yellow panel and the tail is forked. The female is not as brightly coloured. 15 cm.

What they eat Seeds, berries, nuts and buds, and also insects when feeding young. They love to visit birdfeeders for peanuts and sunflower seeds.

Female

Did you know?
Greenfinches are great to watch at birdfeeders. They often squabble and won't think twice about scaring off other birds.

Male

GOLDFINCH
CARDUELIS CARDUELIS

Did you know?

If you leave a weedy area in your garden in which to grow plants such as thistles, you can encourage these beautiful birds to come to your garden.

Juvenile

Adult

When to see All year round.

Where to see Gardens, woodland, farmland and coasts.

What to look for A stunning bird that looks like an exotic pet-shop escapee! In flight, the yellow and black wings are very noticeable. The head is a mixture of red, white and black, with a pale-pink pointed bill. 12 cm.

What they eat With its long pointed bill the Goldfinch can reach seeds from plants such as thistles, teasel, dandelions and burdock.

Goldfinches love nyjer and sunflower seeds, and will take them from birdfeeders.

SPOTTED!

You can use the boxes opposite the bird names on this page to tick off the species you have spotted.

Mute Swan	❏	Skylark		❏
Mallard	❏	Carrion Crow		❏
Tufted Duck	❏	Jackdaw		❏
Great Crested Grebe	❏	Sparrowhawk		❏
Grey Heron	❏	Tawny Owl		❏
Osprey	❏	Collared Dove		❏
Moorhen	❏	Feral Pigeon		❏
Coot	❏	House Martin		❏
Avocet	❏	Swift		❏
Curlew	❏	Swallow		❏
Kingfisher	❏	Great Spotted Woodpecker		❏
Greylag Goose	❏	Pied Wagtail		❏
Canada Goose	❏	Dunnock		❏
Cormorant	❏	Wren		❏
Oystercatcher	❏	Robin		❏
Redshank	❏	Blackbird		❏
Black-headed Gull	❏	Song Thrush		❏
Great Black-backed Gull	❏	Chiffchaff		❏
Common Tern	❏	Goldcrest		❏
Sandwich Tern	❏	Long-tailed Tit		❏
Puffin	❏	Blue Tit		❏
Grey Partridge	❏	Great Tit		❏
Red-legged Partridge	❏	Nuthatch		❏
Pheasant	❏	Jay		❏
Common Buzzard	❏	Magpie		❏
Kestrel	❏	Starling		❏
Lapwing	❏	House Sparrow		❏
Cuckoo	❏	Chaffinch		❏
Woodpigeon	❏	Greenfinch		❏
Little Owl	❏	Goldfinch		❏
Meadow Pipit	❏			